Navigating Negativity

PRACTICAL PARENTING STRATEGIES TO REDUCE CONFLICT AND CREATE CALM

SUSAN VAN SCOYOC PH.D.

For Chad who supports my dreams

For Lilah and Jack who inspire me to be my best every day

For all negative kids who need to be understood

CONTENTS

Introduction:

WHY YOUR NEGATIVE CHILD NEEDS YOUR HELP

"My drawing is so bad. I can't make it look right ever!"
— KATHERINE, AGE 4

"We never go the places I want to go!
— ADAM, AGE 7

"I hate soccer; no one ever passes me the ball!"
— CHRIS, AGE 9

"My friends don't want me around. They never laugh at my jokes. I'm just not funny."
— SARAH, AGE 12

"It doesn't matter how much I study; I never do well on my math tests. I'll never get into college!"
— JESSIE, AGE 16

"Why can't we go to Joe's Pizza, this new place is probably going to be gross!"
— DIEGO, AGE 10

The Problem with Negativity

You chose this book because you are worried about your child's negativity... worried and frustrated and scared and angry and guilty and most other scary parent emotions that come to mind. You want to confidently navigate the road to happiness for your child but find yourself without the words or the patience to clear the trail.

Your negative kid seems to:

View life in all-or-nothing terms
Apply rigid rules for self and others about what is "right"
Turn a minor problem into an instant catastrophe
Focus too much on fairness
Be defiant when something doesn't go as planned
Cherry-pick out the bad and disregard the good
Resist trying new things
Give up when something is hard

Despite your best efforts to be positive, to explain why things aren't so bad, or to punish that bad attitude out of your child, you do not see much progress towards positivity. Your child is NOT growing out of negativity. In fact, grumbling seems to have become an instant response for just about everything! With all of that practice focusing on what is wrong, even when your child is trying to look on the bright side, negativity has become the brain's default reply. It is as if the good parts of life just do not register. You and your child are exhausted from such a grumpy, bumpy ride!

The problem with negativity (and why you need to help) is that it impacts every aspect of a child's life. You may notice struggles related to:

Self-confidence
Coping skills
Family relationships

Maintaining friendships

Participation in new activities

Comfort level in unfamiliar situations

Depression

Anxiety

When you think of how your negative child operates in this world, the risk for these problems probably does not surprise you. The downward spiral created by negativity and the resulting lack of confidence and social support can set the stage for mental health problems. In fact, negative thinking is known to be related to depression. Negative thinkers view obstacles as unchangeable and inescapable, and often their fault — quite a roadmap for feeling helpless and out of ideas for success. Just think about how many times your child seems stuck when solving an everyday problem like making a choice, or perhaps uses the words "always" or "never" to communicate how permanent even small troubles feel!

Negativity might also be anxiety in disguise, as rigidity and complaining often mask the fear of failure or trying something new. If your child puts up a big enough fuss about tasting a new food or visiting an unfamiliar place, you might just give up to avoid the conflict. Anxiety wins and reinforces the idea that complaining works. As chronically negative kids get older, they can also lose social support from friends and family because their difficult-to-please attitudes, as you know, can be overwhelming to others. So what is the result of fewer new experiences due to anxiety or social rejection? Kids with negativity can often get written out of the social stories their friends are creating as they move on without your child.

For all of these reasons — self-esteem, coping skills, family relationships, friendships, new adventures, and mental health — the time to help your child with negativity is now.

What Can You Do To Help?

If you want to guide your negative-by-nature child, there are a few things you need to know and do:

1. **Go First**: Your child needs YOU to set the course for positive change, and you are already taking charge by reading this book!

2. **Know the Enemy**: Negative thinkers are just responding to flawed brain data--they are not being negative on purpose. In this book, you will learn to identify just what might be behind that rigid response and discover critical facts about how negative brains work.

3. **Be a Credible Teacher**: You have to know how to reach and teach your child if you want to be viewed as a credible ally in the fight against negativity. Your child has to trust that you are someone who, when the obstacles and annoyances do happen, sees negativity for what it is and can help navigate to less distressing exits. Chapter 3 gives you tips to boost your teaching success rate that apply to all aspects of parenting, not just conquering negativity.

4. **Know What To Do During Conflict and Every Other Minute of the Day**: The two strategy chapters in this book focus not only on what to do when your child is in full meltdown mode but, even more effectively, what to do every other minute of the day! When your child is upset, what you say and do does matter. Frustrated nonverbal messages and critical words just add fuel to a kid's brain that is already on fire with distress and dissatisfaction. You will discover what to say and do instead, including helpful self-talk to best manage your negative emotions too.

   Although knowing how to manage a meltdown is important, the most powerful way to elevate your parenting confidence and secretly tame negativity at the same time is to figure out how to encourage positivity every other minute of the day. What you do with your child when negativity is NOT driving the car is the most important work you will do. Chapter

4 defines strategies you can use right now (and are probably good at already) to help your child tune in a bit more to the positive and leave those tantrums in the rearview mirror. Remember, what you do and say when your child is in a relaxed, teachable state matter the most!

5. **Don't worry about cooperation**: Not cooperating is something your child is already good at, right? Luckily for you and your family, the strategies you will use from this book require little to no agreement from your child. You will be the scout of the road map behind the scenes, quietly navigating to more peaceful paths. Success will come because we have the right person in charge of this adventure — you! Yes, eventually you can offer your child direct ideas for managing frustration independently. When you start tackling negativity by creating a calm environment first, you can avoid the failure and frustration that happens (for parents and kids) when demands are too high, skills are too low, and emotions are too reactive.

If you like to skip ahead, then start with Chapter 4 or check out the last chapter on Frequently Asked Questions for some reassurance that your issues are the same ones faced by many parents with difficult kids. Better yet, start at the beginning, think about how the information fits your family situation, and be patient as you try out the strategies in this book.

You really can navigate the negativity of your household, reduce conflict, and create a calm atmosphere that encourages your child to learn better emotional control. Your credibility and confidence as you take on negativity will show your child just how to let go of those automatic, grouchy responses that have been driving life to no place fun!

About the Author: Why Can I Help?

As an experienced child psychologist, I have met many children who seem hardwired for negativity. Their parents bring them to me for other reasons such as behavior problems, anxiety, depression, family conflict, or an inability to keep friends. With some digging, I often discover negativity as the root of the problem. I see how this one, reflexive thought habit makes kids feel bad about themselves, ruins social activities and friendships, and torments family relationships.

I know all about the strategic planning that goes into even simple trips to the store to avoid the meltdowns that seem to pop up no matter how sunny the day or how happy the mood just minutes beforehand. I hear kids say they hate themselves or that life feels too hard because no matter how much they try, they just can't stay happy and know they make others grumpy too. Negative kids have taught me a lot about just how discouraging and painful it is to have such a grouchy brain and how much they want adults to understand that they are not being difficult on purpose. They want to figure out more positive ways to look at life as much as, if not more than, their caregivers do!

The strategies in this book are the very same ones I teach to families who have come to me for therapy for the past two decades. The information is based on evidence-supported research and refined by my years of clinical experience to make the strategies easy to implement. You don't need to read one more, overwhelming parenting book that only adds to your lack of confidence.

What you learn here is practical and ready to use from the minute you finish a chapter.

You can absolutely take charge of the negativity in your household by using the strategies in this book. With daily hard work to understand your child's brain and resist the temptation to join in the negative road trip, you will show your child just how powerful it can feel not to be bullied by unhelpful thoughts. Over time, your child will get better and better at the flexible thinking needed to combat that go-to grumpy response and try out more positive ways of coping with life's stressors.

The time to help your child with negativity is now!

Read on to start navigating and conquering negativity in your household today.

Remember, no kid cooperation required!

Now You Know

Negativity impacts Every Aspect of My Child's Life

Negative Thinking can be part of Depression and Anxiety

As a Parent, I have to start the Battle against Negativity

My Child needs to know I am a Trustworthy Partner in the Fight

I can successfully Reduce Negativity without my Child's Cooperation

**The Time to Start is Now; the Tools I need
are Here and Ready to Use Today**

Chapter 1:

WHY IS MY CHILD SO NEGATIVE? 3 KEY FACTS FOR UNDERSTANDING YOUR NEGATIVE THINKER

"We all walk on eggshells. It's impossible to keep her happy."

— Mom of Sal, age 12

"He jumps to the most jaw-dropping conclusions! It's as if A equals Z in his mind!"

— Dad of Aaron, age 14

"She says she loves to dance but never wants to practice and fights us going to class."

— Mom of Amy, age 8

"If something isn't perfect it's a disaster. Even not writing her numbers perfectly is cause for a 10-minute meltdown! She is only 4!"

— Mom of Claire, age 4

"She says she hates herself when she can't figure out hard homework the first time she tries. When I reassure her about how smart she is, she just shuts down even more.

Dad of Emma, age 11

It is a question that seems to have no obvious answer..."why is my child so negative about every little thing?"

Fortunately, we know quite a bit about the misguided, twisty paths of the negative brain! When you understand how negative thinkers think, you can parent with more patience and guide your child out of dead-end disappointments towards more reasonable responses to all things unfair and uncomfortable.

Here are the facts you need to know:

Fact 1: Your Child is Not Negative on Purpose.

Fact 2: Negative Thinkers are Often Anxious Thinkers.

Fact 3: Negative Thinkers Rely on Flawed Thought Habits.

FACT ONE:
Your Child is Not Negative on Purpose

Negative kids are hardwired to notice what is wrong with a situation and respond, as kids do, to the first thought that comes to mind:

It's too hot, too cold, too crunchy, too hard, too soft, too tight, just not right...

It smells weird, looks different, has a brown spot, isn't something I've tried before...

That was unfair, your fault, on purpose, not right, all wrong, won't help, is impossible...

I can't, I'm dumb, it's too hard, I'll do it wrong, why even try...

Kids with negative brains do not see the exit signs for more positive or acceptable options. Their minds go speeding from first sight to most disastrous outcome. A hard math problem zooms right to, "I'm dumb," without braking for any other possibility. A strike out at home plate is now a billboard of failure at all sports. New social experiences are code for Here is Your Chance for Rejection! Such thoughts do not happen on purpose; negativity is its own driver and automatically takes the wheel over and over again during your child's day. The car is low, and even the smallest pebble becomes a pothole of misery.

As children repeatedly magnify the smallest bumps in the road, their brains become better and better at making the connection between experiences and negativity. Time after time, the negative thought arrives first, creating a well-worn and predictable path in the brain, with no apparent, alternative routes. Brain researchers have called this connection "survival of the busiest" (read *The Mind and the Brain* by Schwartz and Begley for more details). For all of us, whatever we do the most, our brain sends resources in that direction, and we get good at that skill or mindset. Our brain doesn't judge. If we practice baking a lot, we master cookies. If we complain a lot, we get good at complaining. The ability to find flaws and fault becomes a habit — brain muscle memory. And what about the path filled with positivity or even just possibility? It hasn't had much traffic in a very long time and may not even show up on the brain GPS.

Is This Your Child?

Think about the last, ten frustrating interactions with your child. Do grumbling replies or meltdowns seem to come automatically? Have you sometimes wondered if those crabby comebacks have become a habit? Have you ever said something like, "You haven't even finished listening to what I am telling you, and you're upset already!"? Pay close attention to your child over the next few days and see if you can detect the automatic nature of negative and out-of-proportion responses to the stressors of daily life. What situations signal the launch into whining? When was it most difficult for your child to exit off that grumbling superhighway? What responses make you think, "Wow, that was too automatic to be on purpose!"?

FACT TWO:
Negative Thinkers are Often
Anxious Thinkers

If you want to help your child get unstuck from negativity, you have to become an expert at recognizing anxiety. Yes, your child could be difficult because of personality hardwiring or a disruptive behavior disorder. But, more often than not, anxiety is also going along for the ride, barking out directions of how to act and what to say when faced with even a hint of uncertainty.

Negativity plus anxiety can look like this:

Has a hard time making decisions
Gives uncaring responses to situations
Seems unaware of the needs of others
Resists trying new things
Avoids new situations, activities, or friendships
Says "I can't" or "It's too hard" when faced with a challenge

These types of responses might come up when you ask your child to choose between two fun activities, do hard homework, practice sports or music, or attend a new social experience. As you are trying to convince your child to see the favorable side of things, the brain only focuses on the possibilities of being uncertain, looking foolish, failing, or regret. Anxiety is behind the wheel, shouting negativity out the window and drowning out your perfectly reasonable point of view.

Let me share an example of anxiety masking itself as negativity:

> When one of my 10-year-old patients heard she had to go to her grandmother's funeral, she promptly proclaimed she was not going to dress up and must be allowed to play on her tablet during the event. She was so flooded with anxiety about

attending her first funeral of a loved one that what came out seemed horribly self-centered and uncaring. Fortunately, her parents knew fear was behind the wheel and did not react by punishing her words. They did not lecture her about acceptable behavior or argue with her about what one wears to a funeral. Instead, they empathized with her fear, waited for her to regain her relaxed mood, then gave her more information about what to expect at the funeral. The next day, even though she didn't like it, she wore her dress clothes and followed the rules about the amount of screen time — with a little grumbling on the side, of course.

Is This Your Child?

What would you say about how your child responds to unfamiliar situations? Challenges? The intense emotional needs of others? Have you sometimes been dumbfounded about how selfish your child seems in a situation? Do you find yourself continually reassuring your child about the awesomeness or safety of a new experience? Do you sometimes think you should buy a pair of pom-poms because are you feel like you're a cheerleader, trying to convince your child that homework, taekwondo moves, music scales, or swimming dives are doable with just a little more practice? Are you exhausted trying to avoid experiences that might seem too different or too hard?

Next time you hear negativity coming from your child, take a minute to strip away the content of the words and see if you can detect anxiety at the core. Consider taking some notes as your child gives you plenty of examples on a particularly rough day. Even more importantly — what areas of life does your child approach with gusto and confidence? You can use all of this information later as you discover strategies to help your negative thinker in the next few chapters.

FACT THREE:
Negative Thinkers Rely on
Flawed Thought Habits

How negative thinkers respond to life is not only reflexive and often driven by anxiety, but is also flawed and unhelpful. Reasonable connections between experiences and responses are almost invisible to a negative thinker, especially in areas of life where your child lacks confidence, is inexperienced, or feels overwhelmed. The error-filled thought habits of negative thinkers mean they are quick to notice the bad and ugly and even quicker to dismiss the good.

This thought habit is why all of the reasoning and reassuring you do does not help.

Those messages do not support the (faulty) evidence the brain is used to, so they fall by the wayside. The brain engages in a misleading loop of automatically finding what is wrong with a situation, then only considering thoughts to support its case. To outsiders, such quick responses seem ridiculous and impulsive but are actually protective and comfortable to the brain paths of a negative child. Remember, your child's brain has well-connected pathways for negativity but the routes for considering positive information have not had much traffic and are not easily accessible.

Take a look at three types of unhelpful thinking patterns below and consider how many sounds just like your child:

Type 1: All-or-nothing

All-or-nothing thinkers interpret situations with a black-and-white mindset. They apply a very rigid set of rules about how life "should" be, especially as it applies to others! Life is lived teetering on the extreme edges of "always" and "never." Negative thinkers lose their emotional balance quickly and often as life does not play by their rules. Such thinkers have a difficult time considering the suggestions of others and are in an almost constant state of disappointment. There is only one right way to do something, and every other way is wrong.

Black-and-white thinking reminds me a lot of the high-achieving patients I see who face an academic challenge. Such kids are either "smart" or "dumb" in their minds, depending on their grades. One difficult multiplication problem and suddenly I am no good at math. No sense trying to convince me otherwise, or bothering to help me with my homework. One young patient I had would not read out loud in front of his teacher or parents until he was sure he could say all of the words. For him, he was only good at reading if he didn't have to sound out any of the words. Of course, the all-or-nothing mindset doesn't just apply to academics. Kids can be rigid about anything that challenges their sense of self.

When thinking is so inflexible, much of what happens in life feels like a catastrophe! If you think in extremes, it is hard to keep your problems the right size. Being wrong, being embarrassed, being uncomfortable, being challenged, or being frustrated all equal a crisis. In fact, any input coming into the brain that does not feel 100% right equals a disaster!

You might be familiar with these examples of all-or-nothing thinking in your child:

The day at the amusement park was either all fun or wholly ruined.

I make a basket in every game, or I am terrible at sports.

If my homework does not look super easy, it is impossible for me to do on my own.

My friends didn't text me back, so they hate me.

One bad grade on my science project means I am dumb.

I get to go to my favorite store first, or shopping with you is a waste of time.

> If I can't play all morning with my friends, I never get to do what I want to do.

> My girlfriend broke up with me so no one will ever like me again.

When all-or-nothing thinking is in charge, even the most caring and reassuring parents often cannot seem to make an impact. All-or-nothing thinking keeps life predictable for negative thinkers, which calms the anxiety that comes along with having such a bossy brain. Unfortunately, such rigid thinking also leads to lots of unpleasant feedback from parents, siblings, coaches, and peers who refuse to play by such unreasonable rules.

Type 2: The Negative Filter

As you know, contrary thinkers are masters at rooting out even the smallest, unpleasant part of a situation, no matter how insignificant or, frankly, nonexistent to the rest of us. The only available exits that pop up on the negative highway are unfairness, blame, disappointment, and uncertainty. Not only does the negative filter magnify even the most remote possibility of a bad outcome, but it is also very loud. The brain becomes filled with the unjust, making it hard to keep perspective on a situation, and even harder to hear your reasons why things are not as bad as they seem at the moment.

Perhaps you have heard your child say things like:

> "You always give her a bigger piece than me!"

> "It's not fair that we have to run errands right now!"

> "It's all your fault that I missed watching my TV shows today!"

> "I don't want to go there; they always put too much ketchup on my burger!"

> "She never plays the right way; that is not how you play tag!"

> "That party isn't going to be fun! I will just embarrass myself since I can't swim."

> "This is impossible! I'm never going to figure out this geometry problem!"

Your child's negative filter clogs the brain, leaving no room for more likely possibilities. This unhelpful filter is why the reassuring, "look at the bright side" speeches you give on a daily basis just don't work. In fact, your efforts to convince your child otherwise may be resulting in a tighter grip on what is wrong with a situation. In the next chapters, you will learn how you can respond to loosen that grip and, without necessarily agreeing with your child, convey an understanding of just how full that negative filter is today.

Type 3: End of the Story

Negative thinkers are also excellent at jumping to conclusions and writing the end of the story before it even happens! They erroneously rely on their fortune-telling skills to predict the outcome of future events. Guess what? The result is never good! Along with sharp fortune-telling skills, negative thinkers are also excellent mind readers. They know exactly what others are thinking (also never positive, by the way) and behave accordingly to support the end of THAT story as well. You can probably guess that by writing the end of the story, negative thinkers can control their anxiety about uncertainty because they now feel sure about what is going to happen, even if it is terrible. This is a common thought habit for my teenage patients, especially when it comes to social events. Often, a teen will choose not to go to dance or try out for an activity because they are sure something awkward will happen.

Typical predictions you might hear from your child could be:

This new pizza place is going to be gross.

The trampoline park is going to be too crowded to be fun.

I just know she didn't text me back because she is tired of me.

Why go to the Homecoming party? People will just laugh at me when I try to dance.

This chore is going to take up way too much time and is way too hard for me!

I'll just mess up if I try out for jazz band, plus the band director hates me!

The bottom line is that the unhelpful thought habit of writing the end of the story changes your child's life story. Kids who live in a world of fortune telling and mind reading don't operate based on what is real and avoid unknown adventures that might help them grow. Predicting the worst turns off peers, resulting in conflict and isolation as trying to convince your negative child that other options exist is just too draining for friends to bother. Some of my patients as young as third grade tell me that their friends complain about how they "bring everyone down" or admit that an invitation to a sleepover was not extended because, "it's too hard to make me happy."

These facts are hard to know as a parent.

Is this your child?

Take some time to think about which of these facts fit your child. If you don't know, take a week and just watch. Make a note of triggers that send that negativity car careening out of control. Watch for when your child seems to respond with a right-sized reaction, too. Both responses will help you understand when your child feels vulnerable instead of comfortable. When you know your child's emotional map, you can better determine which of life's stressors are manageable and which will likely need your support and direction.

How about you? What does your exit habit look like when facing fear, uncertainty, or frustration? Pay extra close attention to your responses to your child. Does your anxiety about their overreaction on the basketball court kick in your negativity pace car as well — "you embarrass me when you are such a poor sport during basketball games!"? What about other caregivers in the home? How do they respond to life's misadventures? You are the role model for keeping problems in perspective and your child is watching.

So how can you use this information? Knowing your child's negative responses are automatic can help you put the brakes on your knee-jerk reaction of anger, arguing, or reasoning in response to the out-of-control ride. And knowing your child is struggling with anxiety and not just being difficult can help you respond with less irritation and more understanding. Your child needs you to know you can slow the journey down and help in finding other exits instead of adding miles to the irritable adventure of the day.

Now that you are more aware of how your child's negative brain works, read on to discover the best ways to be a credible teacher to your child, and to discover strategies to decrease your child's negativity, increase your parenting confidence and create a more relaxed and enjoyable family environment.

The best part of this whole transformation? No kid cooperation required!

<u>Now You Know</u>

Negative Thoughts are Automatic and Not on Purpose

Negativity just might be Anxiety in Disguise

My Child might view Life in All-or-Nothing Terms

A Negative Filter does not let Positive Thoughts Get In

Writing the End of the Story is a Protection Against Uncertainty

My Child's Negative Story is Changing Life's Story

It is My Job to Truly Understand how My Child Thinks

Chapter 2:

HOW TO REACH AND TEACH YOUR NEGATIVE THINKER

"Kids do well if they can."

— ROSS W. GREENE, PH.D., AUTHOR OF *RAISING HUMAN BEINGS: CREATING A COLLABORATIVE PARTNERSHIP WITH YOUR CHILD*

"The goal is not to make your child get defensive about his negativity but to gain some distance from it."

— TAMAR CHANSKY, PH.D., AUTHOR OF *FREEING YOUR CHILD FROM NEGATIVE THINKING*

"Our kids are not manipulating us; in part, they're expressing what we train them to do."

— ALAN KAZDIN, PH.D., AUTHOR OF *THE KAZDIN METHOD FOR PARENTING THE DEFIANT CHILD*

"I have no idea what I am doing!"

Parent sentiments such as this are often expressed in my office. All parents feel like this from time to time, myself included, when the strategies we are using to reach and teach our children seem to wind up at the same, maddening dead end. No matter how hard we try, we just can't seem to "make" our child listen, behave, be positive, be flexible, be brave, or be that little person who goes with the flow and joyfully accepts all of our wise advice.

Yet down that same road we travel, again and again, armed with unhelpful road signs like, "how many times do I have to tell you," "this is ridiculous," and "This.Is.Not.That.Big.Of.A.Deal!" We foolishly expect a different result that never comes and end up feeling defeated and guilty.

Before you can truly help your child loosen that firm hold on negativity and create a calmer household, you have to capitalize on what you can control — you!

If you want successful change in your household, you have to go first. Period. As you already know from the battles with negativity you have already survived, what doesn't work is expecting your oppositional child to go first or to figure it out alone.

A child who is not open to change, does not like new things, has a knack for noting disaster, and has poor emotional control is a terrible person to put in charge of this adventure!

Your child may not grow out of negativity. This is why you have to put deliberate effort into teaching ways to fight back against the automatic grouchiness and flawed thinking habits that have become a mental habit. You have to add exits to your child's emotional highway and be the GPS needed to find them.

Before you start using the negativity-busting strategies in the next chapters, here are four essential tips that will help you reach and teach your child successfully:

1. **Biology Matters:** Kids can't focus on learning new skills when they are tired, hungry, or on sensory overload.

2. **Thinking vs. Feeling**: Kids can't problem solve well when emotions are high.

3. **Start Where You Need to Start**: Start where your child is in managing emotions, not where you think such skills "should" be.

4. **Be Patient.** New habits take a long time to develop and use, especially under stress.

Tip 1. Biology Matters

The basics count when it comes to your ability to teach and your child's ability to learn.

By basics, I mean the necessary elements of predictability, comfort, food, and sleep that we all need to perform our best work. If your child's schedule is uncertain, learning diverts to making sense of the day. If your child is in pain, ill, hungry, or tired, problem solving will take a backseat to the search for comfort. And what about you? If you are hungry or stressed, you are more likely to be impatient and forget your goals of teaching your child how to get through frustrations without a meltdown.

By design, our bodies are driven to focus on our primary needs and divert our brain power in that direction to meet those needs first. Biology and stress can create a pothole into an otherwise smooth road for the day, kicking in that default, negative highway for you and your child.

Of course, you cannot always prevent illness, pain, after-school hunger, or disrupted sleep schedules. Just know that when your child's biology is a mess, you may have to modify expectations for coping with stressors.

Think about what small steps you can take to make sure biology is not interfering with your child's ability to handle the frustrations of the day. Can you stick to that morning schedule? Have a snack waiting in the car for after school pick up? Avoid long shopping trips at nap time? Be more consistent with the bedtime routine? Give your teen a break from chores during finals week? Help with homework after you have a snack, too?

Respecting your child's biological needs is ok. In fact, it is more than ok; it is brilliant parenting! Not only does it allow your child to be in a ready-to-learn state, but it also helps you teach your child the importance of self-care such as eating and getting enough sleep.

Therapist Note on Sensory Issues: Many children also struggle with sensory overload that can make learning new things a challenge. Your child may have meltdowns over seams in socks, scratchy underwear, loud environments, or smelly food. Kids with such sensitivities experience life with overwhelming intensity and retaliate strongly when they feel bombarded by their environments, which can happen often.

As a teacher, you will have to tread lightly when negativity seems rooted in sensory dysregulation; handle such environmental sensitivities once you and your child have made some progress in other areas of life. For example, if your child has meltdowns about getting dressed, don't expect progress on this issue just because you are staying calm instead of arguing about t-shirt softness. Start with homework, chores, fairness of board games, or any other topic that does not combine negative hardwiring with sensory glitches. If you are concerned about the role sensory regulation plays in your child's overall functioning, please contact your healthcare provider for referrals to a behavioral therapist or an occupational therapist who may be able to help.

Tip 2. Thinking vs. Feeling

When we take in information, one of two parts of our brain is mostly in charge — thinking or feeling. The thinking brain takes the reins when we are relaxed, not feeling threatened, and focused on the task at hand. The feeling side of our brain, on the other hand, is wired to add emotional meaning to the information so we know whether we should be scared, stressed, happy, excited, or some combination of feelings. Unfortunately for your child, that emotional brain tends to hijack daily situations without reason. Instead of being able to act on facts ("I have homework"), your child's brain acts on emotion and flawed conclusions ("I hate homework!" "It's too hard!" "I am dumb at math!" "I'll never get this done!").

Think about how cloudy your head is when you are stressed. You are likely forgetful, irritable, and poorly focused. When your child is upset or stuck in a negative loop, thinking clearly and hearing what you are trying to say just isn't happening. Many parents launch into their most impressive lectures when their child is upset and demanding, perhaps thinking that is the time to talk some sense into their stubborn offspring. If that worked, you would not need this book.

Trying to teach your child new skills while either one of you is upset is a waste of time. Worse than that? It is a credibility destroyer.

When your child is emotional, the thinking brain is not available to process the information you are trying to share. If you are agitated too, fuel is added to the fire as your confused child tries to balance surging inner emotions with your intense mood and words. Your child is focusing on escaping this stressful exchange, not on ways to problem solve or calm down.

Take a minute and think about the last heated exchange you had with your child. Did the situation escalate as you tried to first calmly reason and then lose your cool? Did you end up saying things you wish you hadn't said as your child shut down or ramped up? Do you secretly equate having the last word with your child as being the "winner" of the argument?

If you want to teach skills to minimize negativity, you have to wait until your child is teachable — when the thinking part of the brain is in charge. If you want to be a credible teacher, you also have to consider your delivery and avoid any unhelpful parenting habits such as yelling and belittling that sparks the emotional brain and sends it back to the front line — more about this in the next chapter.

For now, watch out for when your child's emotions are in charge and do your best to disengage. You are not letting your child "win", you are merely being smart about your timing and mindful of just what part of the brain is driving the car.

Tip 3. Start Where You Need to Start

Change is successful when you start where you need to start. If you are going grocery shopping, you figure out your list, make sure you have money, and target the aisles you need to pick up your items. You don't go the cashier first and demand to know how much you owe for your groceries that are still on the shelves!

You start where you need to start.

The same is true when trying to teach your child anything, but especially when trying to teach self-regulation skills like managing negativity. You will need to become a master at figuring out where your child is as well as the most useful emotional destination.

For example, you would love for your child to pick up toys with a cheerful, "Sure mom, would love to help out!" Right now, however, any request for chores results in instant fussing about unfairness and that the job is too hard! The strategies in the next chapter will help you figure out how empathizing ("I can tell your brain thinks this is a huge job!") and helping your child get the task done ("I'll do this half") can ultimately break that cycle of negativity, arguing, and exasperation.

When relaxed conditions are in place, your child does not have to hang on to negativity so hard, is more cooperative, and learns not only to override those negative messages but also how to complete effortful tasks.

But wait, you might be thinking-doesn't this mean I am giving in to my child by lowering my expectations?

Ultimately, starting where you need to start just means being respectful of your child's limits and setting the stage for successful teaching. It does not mean giving up on the idea that your child will be able to independently clean a room, do homework, or be open to new experiences. It does not mean clearing all of the landmines that might set off an emotional explosion. You can have the same life skill expectations; you just have to alter the schedule of how long it will take your child to meet them.

Starting where you need to start is not easy. Your own anxiety may push you to ineffectively scold and give consequences to your child for not responding in the "should" range. "My ten-year old should be able to eat toast without always complaining about the crust!" or, "My 14-year-old should be able to do chores without whining about how hard they are." Sound familiar?

If you think about it, there are probably many situations where you, as an adult, also "should" be able to be successful but are not — quitting a habit, exercising, eating right, or mastering your cell phone camera. For

ANYONE trying to learn something new, the most success happens when you start small and build from there.

The reminding, coaxing, and reprimanding you may do now for the "should" does not work. You are reading this book so you can try something different—parenting strategies that are more successful. Gradually shaping your child's reactions to emotional situations is one of those strategies.

How about you? How many times in a day do you think or say the word "should" concerning your child? How would you rank this as a source of frustration? Try a day without using the word "should" out loud or in your brain. Spend some time figuring out just where your child is and what your ultimate goal is for flexibility and frustration tolerance. Play around with helping your child out a little more and yelling a little less. See if you can break that cycle of demand, disappointment, negativity, and tears.

Tip 4. Be Patient

Think about what it took for your child to learn to walk, to read, or to ride a bike. Lots of patience and lots of practice, right?

Learning how to be less pessimistic and reactive are skills too, no different than learning to write your name.

It will take your child some time to figure out other ways to respond to stressful events besides getting upset, complaining or arguing. Remember, negative thoughts pop into your child's mind automatically and their brain holds on tight to irrational evidence. Your child isn't purposefully picking the darkness of a pancake or how long it will take at the grocery store as stressful events — the negative brain hijacks such experiences and spits out the grumbles!

If you can view your child's struggles with negativity as simply a self-regulation skill they have yet to master, you will be more patient with the process.

You will become a credible teacher in your child's eyes — someone who can help — instead of a co-pilot who seems to be careening out of control as well.

When you are patient, you create a relaxed learning environment. Your child can then more easily discover how to recognize negative thoughts as untrue and unhelpful. And over time, with your help, their brain will generate more useful ways to respond to life's bumps. By the way, situations that already trigger a fierce negative response require more patience and practice. For example, if running errands right after school always triggers a meltdown, you can expect that your child will be resistant to being flexible with that situation. Even greater tolerance will be necessary when stressors are piled up on your child such as poor sleep, being hungry, traveling, a change in routine, starting a new school year, or persistent social problems. Keep quick triggers and stress in mind when you are figuring out which life events might be the most difficult to change for your child right now. Then start someplace easier.

You also have to be patient with yourself as learning new ways to think about and respond to your child is hard. You have also had a lot of practice responding in ways that may not be as effective as you would like them to be when it comes to your child's emotional dysregulation. You might also find yourself falling back into yelling or belittling when tensions are high. This is normal and expected. Keep practicing and focusing on making proactive, mindful choices about how your respond to your child instead of reactive ones that discourage learning and decrease your parenting confidence.

The next chapters will help you learn ways to behave and talk to yourself that can help you be more unruffled with your child, increasing confidence that you are doing the right things to build the positive inroads your child needs to be less negative.

<u>Now You Know</u>

If I Want Change in My Home, I have to Go First

My Child can Learn Better when Fed, Rested, and Relaxed

**Trying to Teach My Child when Emotions
are In Charge Does Not Work**

My High Emotional State only Confuses My Child

Setting My Expectations to Fit My Child does not mean I am Giving In

Teaching is about Starting at the Beginning, Timing, and Patience

Chapter 3:

PARENT CONFIDENTLY WHEN NEGATIVITY IS IN CHARGE

"Why does Janie always get the red cup, you know that one is my favorite!"

— JACK, AGE 7

"This second problem is too hard; I hate math!"

— RIDLEY, AGE 12

"If that roller coaster was not closed, this day might have actually been fun!"

— JOSE, AGE 14

"I knew I should not have picked going to a movie with grandma! I would have had so much more fun at Jenny's party. I always pick wrong!"

— SAL, AGE 13

"I struck out on purpose! I told you I was not good at baseball!"

— CONNOR, AGE 10

Now that you have read the previous chapters, you know why your child defaults to the negative road and what you need to do to build your credibility as a tour guide, gently redirecting that path. This chapter will teach you more specific strategies you can start today to confidently throw in a positive detour when pessimism is calling the shots.

Let me remind you of the best part!

None of the strategies you learn about in this book require your child's cooperation and all of them lay the foundation for improving your child's emotional regulation (not just taming negativity). Other welcome side effects of these strategies include reducing your guilt and increasing calm in your household as you gain more confidence in dealing with your challenging child.

The strategies in this chapter focus on what to do when your child is in the midst of a cranky crusade.

First, let's get rid of what does not work — the reassuring, reasoning, arguing, and scolding you use when your frustration boils over. I start here because it can be easier to stop doing something than it can be to add a new, unfamiliar skill. As you are mastering what not to do, you will learn what to say and do when your child is upset. You will also learn helpful ways to talk to yourself when your child's irritability tries to boss you around too.

Important Disclaimer: The strategies in this chapter are essential for reducing the intensity of the conflict in your household, but are not necessarily designed to teach your child how to be more flexible and optimistic. Those skills develop best when the environment is calm and nonthreatening, not in the middle of a bickering battle. The next chapter will show you how to engage in meaningful teaching every other minute of the day when your child is not upset! For now, let's focus on smoothing out the bumpy rides.

Setting the Stage

To become a credible teacher in your child's eyes, you have to stop what doesn't help, practice what works and have the patience to move your child's mindset centimeter by centimeter towards a less automated response to stress. Just remember it may be as hard for your child to consider positive options as it would be for you to become a pessimistic grump. If you are already a pessimistic grump, then you are living proof of how much work it can be to change your wiring!

Before you use the strategies in this chapter, remember these five important facts you learned previously in this book:

1. My child is not negative on purpose.

2. Negative thoughts for my child are automatic and flawed.

3. My child learns best when emotions, especially anxiety, are not in charge—mine or my child's.

4. I am not "giving in" to my child when I respect biological and emotional limits. I am a wise parent.

5. It will take time for my child and me to learn new ways of responding to life's stressors and each other.

A warning that changing how you respond to your child may feel unnatural at first. Reacting in different ways is uncomfortable and takes practice no matter how old you are. You are also learning new skills and are at risk of falling back into your old, unhelpful habits when you are under stress. Repeat the above facts when you are having a hard time with your child's negativity. Post these facts in your phone's notes, on your pantry door and in your underwear drawer to remind you of how important your mindset is when trying to help your child.

Your child needs you to remember.

Strategy One: What Not To Say

Here are some ways you might be responding to your grumbling child that are not helpful, and in fact are encouraging your child to hold on tightly to negative thinking:

REASONING

"It's only an hour long trip. Then you will get to play with your friends."

"It's your Papa's birthday and this is his favorite restaurant so try it for him."

"You like other kinds of pasta, so I am sure you will like the noodles here."

"Everyone makes mistakes when they start out."

REASSURING

"This isn't so bad!"

"You are so good at this, why don't you want to practice to get even better?"

"All of your friends will be there so you will have fun at the new park!"

"Nobody makes a basket every time!"

"Math is easy for you if you take some time to think about it."

SCOLDING

"Stop complaining!"

"I've told you 100 times we are not going!"

"This is not a big deal, stop whining!"

"After all of the fun we have had today, I can't believe you are mad about that!"

"You never listen the first time!"

BELITTLING

"You are never happy with anything!"

"Why do I even buy you things? You never like them!"

"What are you complaining about this time?"

"You are ridiculous!"

"You are ruining this for the whole family!"

"What is your problem?"

ARGUING

"How many times have I told you we are not going to get ice cream?"

"No, you will listen to me!"

"For the last time, we are not going to the store!"

"This is the last time I am arguing with you about that!"

THREATENING

"If you don't stop complaining, I am going to take away your..."

"I'll give you something to really cry about!"

"One more word about it and I will..."

Sound familiar? When you respond negatively to negativity, the main thing you accomplish is two cranky people who feel the need to hold on tighter and tighter to their side of the story. Have you noticed that the more you argue, the more your child gets to practice telling you additional, often dumbfounding, evidence for that cynical point of view? It's as if your unhelpful words fuel your child's negative ride.

And when you try too hard to reason or reassure, your irritable child does not feel heard and does not believe you anyway. For example, I have had countless parents tell me they try to reassure and reason with their kids for hours about how easy homework will be that night, only to be met with more and more resistance and protests of, "that is not how my teacher said to do it!" In reality, if your child could consider all of those positive factors you are selling, negativity would not be a problem in the first place! As you have discovered, throwing rational information at an irrational child does not work.

SIDE EFFECTS WARNING: Perhaps the most alarming side effect of unhelpful responses is that they reinforce your child's belief that the problem is, indeed, a big one. Otherwise, why would a grownup such as you be getting so emotionally worked up too? Why would you resort to such hurtful words if the situation was manageable? Why would you add to the shame already felt by pointing out how easy it "should" be to do or feel differently? From your child's perspective, you not only misunderstand the distress but you don't even know how to help when needed most!

As you learned in the previous chapter, the bottom line is when your child is negative or upset, the side of the brain that solves problems effectively is not in charge. The wrong words not only confuse and irritate, but also cause your child to flee emotionally to escape the intensity of the exchange. As one of my young patients so poignantly shared with me, "I can't hear when my dad yells at me!" Yes, there is a time and place for presenting reasonable options and encouragement but not as a response to a meltdown.

Another side effect of your unhelpful responses is parental guilt. When you get angry at your child for negativity, you might say some hurtful things. The guilt you feel for blowing your cool can make it harder for you to set limits later in the day. After all, you both just had a major meltdown. Who wants to go through that twice in one day? A vicious cycle of guilt and giving in is created, fueling your parenting uncertainty and adding to your child's confusion. Keeping your cool is just as crucial for your mental health as it is for your child's!

So if you should not reason, reassure, scold, belittle, argue, or threaten, what should you say or do instead?

Strategy Two: What To Say Instead

When your child is upset, the words you say either enrage or help to calm. Your goal is to help your child feel heard, perhaps understood, and to avoid the escalation that can quickly occur with your intense response. The whole problem does not have to be solved in an instant. You first task is to merely slow down the runaway car. The time for considering alternative routes on the map comes later when emotions are not in charge.

Here are some responses, delivered in a matter-of-fact tone, that tell your upset child you are confidently dialed into the dilemma and know it is manageable:

"Sounds like you are mad."

"I wish it were different too."

"It's hard to leave when you are having so much fun."

"Wow, this problem must feel enormous!"

"I can tell this is really bothering you."

"Seems like your brain thinks this is how you are going to feel forever."

"Sometimes new things can feel creepy at first."

"I am going to take a walk so we can stop arguing about this."

"Your brain only noticed the bad parts of today, huh?"

"I can tell your brain is writing the end of this story before we even know what it is."

"I know you wanted that to feel fairer."

As you can tell from these statements, you are simply making an observation. You are neutral, supportive, and keeping the problem the right size. You are responding with empathy to the struggle of your child's brain and not the content of the words. You are not agreeing to stay ten more minutes at the park because your child is whining; you are just recognizing that it is hard to leave a fun time. You are not giving your child a laundry list of all the reasons why math should be easy; you are acknowledging that brains sometimes forget what we are good at when something looks hard.

The right words cut down your child's need to be defensive.

The right words lend credibility to you and to the idea that maybe this feeling is temporary and maybe there are other ways to feel about this situation. Your ability to deliver the right words in a confident, matter-of-fact way tells your child this is not a crisis.

Here is the hard part: You have to master a mix of what to say and when to say it (with a dash of silence) for as long as your child is upset. If you blow up or move to reasoning after ten minutes of trying to be neutral, you will be just like a slot machine that paid off a winning hand. These responses will only reinforce your child's instinct to whine and complain until the brain gets the reinforcement it's expecting: proof that this situation is, indeed, a big deal!

If your child's persistence triggers a temper tantrum of your own, take a break, go in a different room, or suggest your child find something relaxing to do away from you. Let your child know this is why you are not going to respond anymore — to stop negativity from bossing you both around. It will take some time but the better you get at not engaging your child, the better your child will get at letting go of negativity and the intense emotions that go along for the ride.

Therapist Tip: If ALL words seem to add fuel to your child's emotional fire, a kiss on the head, quick back rub, or side squeeze or just walking away may be all you can do to help your child calm down. If your child protests with a snippy response, just ignore it. Comebacks from you such as, "I'm just trying to help!" or "Fine, stay miserable!" are not helpful.

The bottom line is your child's responses are reflexive and irrational, so yours have to be deliberate and thoughtful. Your job is to respond to your child's skill deficit of seeing positive options, not to the ugly words that come out when stress is in charge.

Strategies One and Two in Action:

You now have a better idea of what not to say and what to say instead when your child is whiny, cranky, and complaining. Read through the common scenarios below to see these strategies in action:

Child: "This whole day was ruined! I can't believe the Thunder Ride was closed!"

Instead of: "Nothing is ever good enough for you! You are so ungrateful! We are never coming back here again!"

Try This: "I know that is your favorite ride. How frustrating it was closed."

Child: "I am not going to Pizza Joe's! I don't even know what kind of cheese they use!"

Instead of: "You are so picky! This isn't about you; I want to go here!"

Try This: "New places can feel weird sometimes. You can have something to eat when you get home if you don't like it."

Child: "I will never be good at dance! Everyone could see how terrible I did at rehearsal today!"

Instead of: "What do you mean? You are an awesome dancer! You will get it next time!"

Try This: "I can tell your brain thinks that you will never figure out that dance move."

Child: "You always make me do too many chores!"

Instead of: "Keep complaining and I will give you ten more!"

Try This: "Chores do feel too big sometimes. Let me know if you want my help knowing where to start."

Child: "I can't believe you are making me go to my sister's game, now I won't have any time to play!"

Instead of: "Are you kidding me? She goes to all of your events and never complains!"

Try This: "Sounds like you are worried about having some downtime this week."

Child: "I will never learn how to open my locker! I got the worst one at school!"

Instead of: "Everyone else has figured it out, I am sure you are smart enough to get it."

Try This: "These first days are overwhelming. Do you want my help or are you just venting?"

If you read through these more neutral responses, you can feel the energy change.

Your child will have very little to fight back against or hold onto as you agree with the emotion of the situation and not the content of the words.

Strategy Three: Managing Your Own Emotions

One of the hardest and most critical challenges in parenting is managing your own emotions as your child's behavior pushes your buttons. Negativity is an expert irritability activator for all parents! Additionally, your worries and pessimism about your child's skills can result in defeated self-talk about just how capable your child is for overcoming negative thinking.

Here are some examples of unhelpful, parent self-talk:

"I can't stand this!"

"I know she is just trying to ruin my day!"

"He always acts like a jerk around my parents!"

"What if he never makes any friends?"

"She just can't handle this type of change!"

"He can't ever catch a break!"

"I'm so worried he actually hates himself."

As you can tell, these types of statements only feed your negative emotions and paralyze you with fear about how your child will turn out. Such worries might lead you to limit your child's exposure to distress or failure. The parent of one of my patients told me she could not help but picture her tantrum-prone three-year-old as a teenager with no friends because she always had to have her own way. Yet, despite this worrisome image, she often gave in to her demands because she felt guilty about being at work all day. It isn't hard to see from this example and perhaps in your own responses how the cycle of negativity can be reinforced.

Helpful self-talk, on the other hand, can give you the patience and stamina you need to cope with your child's challenging behavior. Below are some useful phrases you can say to yourself in order to not lose your cool and to stay off your child's negative superhighway:

"My child is not doing this on purpose."

"My child is simply not skilled at handling stress, nothing more."

"I do not need to respond like this is an emergency."

"I don't have to be bossed around by negativity just because my child is."

"I need to show my child that these feelings are temporary and manageable."

"If I treat this outburst like it is a crisis, my child will feel that way too."

"Will this response help my child learn coping skills or will it show that I will give in to constant whining?"

"My child is not trying to make me look bad."

"Just because my child acts like this does not mean I am a bad parent."

"My child can handle this problem with my help."

"Adversity is not a bad thing; this situation will help my child grow."

Which of those statements sounds like something you could tell yourself? Do you need to remember that your child simply lacks self-regulation skills? Is it key for you to recognize that most situations are not the emergencies you make them out to be? Do you think your child is trying to hurt your feelings intentionally?

Take time to write down the most challenging situations with your child. Then write down not only the thoughts you can tell yourself in your head but what you also might say out loud to your child. The reason for this exercise is that it is difficult for you to think clearly when you are upset, just like it is for your child. By generating a "cheat sheet" when you are calm and thoughtful, you can generate some solid ideas on what helps the most. The bottom line is you cannot match the emotional intensity of your child or this negativity cycle at your house will not end.

Therapist Note: If you find that your personal history, mental or physical illness, family stressors, or a personality mismatch make it difficult for you avoid hurtful words towards your child or yourself, please consider seeking outside mental health help for yourself, your family, or both. The wait for a skilled therapist can be long so make an appointment as soon as you think it is a good idea and don't wait for your family problems to get worse. You can always cancel the appointment if your situation improves.

You have to believe that you and your child are tough enough to fight back against negativity. You have to be an empathic, confident bystander who will not go along for the ride. Your child is looking to you for how big to feel about the situation and needs you to keep it the right size. When you respond to the facts and not emotions (yours or your child's), your child will trust you more, defenses will go down, and the door will open a crack for those teachable moments to sneak in.

It can be overwhelming to know what you have to do differently to help your negative child so here is some good news: You can actually do your best parenting work when it is easier — when your child is calm or at least neutral. The next chapter gives you the real power tools—easy-to-implement ideas for creating habits of positivity in your home for all of those minutes when your child is not a cranky mess. Read on!

Now You Know

I Can't Expect my Child to be Good at Managing Stress if I Am Not

**Reasoning and Reassuring Don't Sound
Believable when My Child is Upset**

Hurtful Words only Fuel my Negative Child

What I Say to my Child is Vital for Calming Emotions

**What I Say to Myself is Even More Important
for Calming Everyone's Emotions**

Chapter 4:

PARENTING FOR EVERY OTHER MINUTE OF THE DAY: YOUR MOST POWERFUL STRATEGIES FOR CREATING CALM

"It's true. How can I expect my son to stop complaining when that's all he hears from me?"

— MOM OF DIEGO, AGE 9

"I feel better about myself and my son now that I've stopped being so critical of everything."

— DAD OF SAM, AGE 10

"Some days I have to look very hard for the positive, but that is good for me to do as a parent!"

— MOM OF ALEXA, AGE 5

"You can't have so much pride that you refuse to learn new ways to deal with your kid."

— DAD OF EVA, AGE 13

It's time to take a deep, confident breath.

Your best parenting work absolutely happens when your child is the most teachable, and that is not in the heat of an irritable meltdown. The strategies in this chapter allow you to work your magic in the background of your child's day. No cooperation is required because you are not giving your child anything to fight against. Instead of conflict, mindful and meaningful interactions with you and others will build a solid road for positively coping with stressors.

How?

By Modeling what is Right, Noticing what is Good, and Building the Opposite of Negativity.

How you behave is essential when it comes to teaching emotional control to your child — you can't ask your child to act more grown up than you do under stress! You also need to become an expert at noticing the positive minutes of your child's day to change the cycle of conflict in your household. The strategies in this chapter will help you discover creative ways to build the opposite of negativity — ideas for shining a spotlight on gratitude and sharing what's incredible about your child with others.

Here are your ideas for every other minute of the day:

Strategy One: Model What Is Right

You know the adage, "Do as I Say, Not as I Do"? That one is not going to work for helping your child manage intense emotions. As the leading role model for emotion management in in your child's life, you have to be vigilant about how you talk to your child when you are upset and also about what you say out loud about your problems and other people.

For a quick self-test, ask yourself these questions:

Do you use negative, black-and-white talk when interacting with your child?

> Example: "You never do what I ask you to do!"

Do you frequently complain about frustrating situations?

> Example: "My job is the worst; my boss must hate me!"

Do you put yourself down in all-or-nothing terms when you are upset?

> Example: "I am such a terrible cook! Nothing I make on the grill ever turns out right!"

Are you overly negative and critical of other people?

> Example: "Our waitress is terrible! She can't get anything right!"

Your child is watching you and taking mental notes.

One of the most effective ways you can develop your child's positive outlook on life is to improve yours.

Think before you speak. Ask yourself if what you are about to say to or in front of your child has to be said or said right then. Can you wait to vent until after your child has gone to bed? Can you keep those biting words in a thought bubble until the urge to blurt them out passes?

You don't have to pretend that life is never frustrating but you do have to do a better job sending messages that irritating situations are temporary and manageable, like this:

"Doing homework together is frustrating tonight. I will bet we can make it work tomorrow night."

"Well that did not go well, but I will get it right next time!"

"This afternoon was a real drag at work; luckily I have tomorrow off!"

"Our waitress must be super busy to be so forgetful. Next time we will come when it is not so crowded."

"Looks like I need more practice grilling unless I can open a burnt food restaurant somewhere and make lots of money!"

"Losing that paper feels like a big deal right now; I need to calm down and think of some places I might have left it."

If you are negative in your daily interactions with others, are quick to anger over small issues, and expose your child to a chronically critical environment, success will not come easily to your child for managing personal frustration. Your child is watching what exit you take when negative emotions are in charge. You can't ask your child to be better at stress management than you are.

Be vigilant, be thoughtful in your responses, and remember you are the best person to go first.

Strategy Two: Notice What Is Good
USE YOUR WORDS

There is simply no way to minimize what is challenging about your child without broadcasting the message of what is incredible about your child even louder!

If you want your child to notice positive parts of life more often, then spend more time focusing on what is positive about your child. Aim for a ratio of 5 positive to every 1 criticism of your child to help shift attention from what's always wrong to what is even a little bit right about a day. This ratio is supported in the research for not only improving the behavior of children, but for adults in the workplace as well!

Here are some ideas to get you started:

"Thanks for being flexible and trying the new pizza place tonight."

"I know you wanted to ride one more ride; I'm glad your brain didn't get too angry about having to go home."

"Sounds like you are pretty happy with how hard you worked on that project even if the kids in your group didn't work as hard."

"It would have been easy to get stuck on losing that game. You should be proud of how well you handled yourself after the game today."

"That was so helpful when you played quietly on your tablet while I talked to grandma. You are getting so good at being patient!"

"You are turning into such a problem solver! You figured out that if you did your homework right away, you would still have time to play outside this afternoon."

Notice that the comments above are specific and many target the emotion management skills you are trying to build. Skills like flexibility, letting things go, patience, and recognizing that problems are often temporary. Direct and precise comments are much more helpful than the standard, "Good job today, honey!". If your boss let you know that taking the time to go over specific reports with your coworkers contributed to getting the job done efficiently, you would be more likely to keep approaching projects in the same way. If she just said, "Thanks for being a team player" you would not have much of an idea of what she valued in you. The feedback that works for you works for your child too.

Be specific, be sincere, and be generous!

What about the "Yeah, but" monster?

You might be thinking, "I do praise my kid, but all I hear is, 'yeah, but...' and my efforts to be positive don't seem to change anything!" I agree that most negative kids can find ten reasons why you are wrong when you try to point out positives, especially in areas where they feel most vulnerable.

Remember, because of how much the brain has practice being negative, it's as if there are 'road closed' signs on the positive exits, leaving only the option of the negative highway. What can a parent do if there are no detours allowed in a child's negative mind?

The key to making in-roads with this strategy is to start with situations where your child is most likely to accept your positive comments. Avoid praising sports and homework if these areas quickly trigger negativity for your child. Stick with situations your child is already good at and has few reasons to complain.

Consider these ideas:

A flexible choice between purchasing two preferred toys

Agreeing to a type of cereal that was their second choice for breakfast

Mastering a level on a video game

Creating a unique world on a tablet game

Allowing a friend to choose which movie to watch at a sleepover

Helping you with preferred tasks such as washing your car or baking cookies

If positive comments in such situations still trip your child's negativity radar, wait to deliver the praise until well after the event. By waiting, that impulsive urge to contradict you might be a bit more muted. Waiting also reduces your child's tendency to get upset about choices. Sometimes when you praise your child when options still seem possible ("wait, I actually want that other toy!"), complaining might rear its ugly head yet again! Are you starting the get the sense that timing is everything in parenting?

When Praise Feels Uncomfortable: There are many reasons why praise can feel uncomfortable to you and your child. If there is a long history of conflict or if you have been extremely critical in the past, it might be easier to start with neutral comments instead of positive ones. By loading up on neutral comments, your child begins to trust that the sentiments coming out of your mouth won't be harsh or judgmental. The defensive guard can come down and the possibility of listening to what you have to say increases a little. In fact, neutral comments are a key component of research-based parent training programs like Parent-Child Interaction Therapy.

Neutral comments should be objective observations about events of the day such as:

"I see a lot of green in your painting."
"You and your friends rode far on your bikes today."
"That book you read about space has lots of pages!"
"You made it to the 10th level on your video game."
"You had time to play chess today with your buddies."

The parenting skills of delivering neutral comments and specific praise can be challenging to master.

Many parents tell me it is harder than they thought it would be because, as a parent, you feel like you are supposed to be continually evaluating and teaching your child. But remember, if your child is typically in an irritable state, the windows are rolled up tight, and learning isn't happening anyway. Actually, your child is learning something — interactions are about judging and getting people to see your point of view is the ultimate goal. You can help crack the windows just a little bit by offering neutral comments and positive alternatives that don't trip your child's negativity wire, eventually creating the more open attitude you desire.

Try it for a week. Write down some neutral comments that sound natural to you. Practice on your significant other, co-workers, friends and pets. What positive comments can you offer that are specific? Practice those, too. Then try them out on your child!

GOODS ON PAPER

Words are useful and necessary, but we are also visual creatures who absorb data about our world through our eyes. You can make your positive observations soak in even deeper by adding visual proof:

Good Thing of The Day: Start a visual tally of the good things of the day in a spot your child will see regularly. Tape a piece of paper to the bathroom door, write on the family whiteboard, start a running text message, or hang sticky notes inside the pantry. Every day, write one meaningful thing about the day or draw a picture if your child is young.

Your Note of the Day might say:

> "So glad we had time to read our book together tonight!"
>
> "Sounds like you and your friend had some good laughs about those cat videos!"
>
> "Still laughing about the dog trying to use the treat ball!"
>
> "So yummy to have your favorite pizza for dinner!"
>
> "Really appreciated your help planning dad's birthday party."
>
> "The outfit you picked out was just right for picture day!"

As you can see, the comments can be about your child, routine activities, or simple observations about the day. It is crucial to avoid a heavy focus on the general behavior of your child such as, "you were so good at grandma's today" or outcomes such as, "you got an A on your math paper." Broad statements won't teach your child to be mindful and pay attention to the moments of the day. And outcome statements like a grade on a test are often a cue for more complaining, especially in areas where your child is sensitive to failure. Instead, think of what events might entice your child to notice the other minutes of the day when emotions were not so intense. Your sole goal is to add those positive or even neutral detours, expanding your child's options next time negativity seems like the only road in sight.

Therapist Note: Sometimes parents try to force their child to also add positive comments or notes for the day. If your child is ready to do so, noticing the warm fuzzy parts of others can be a meaningful way to increase personal positivity as well. But if your child complains about trying to think of a good thing for the day, or refuses to do so, it just means the timing is not right, and you have more modeling to do. Do not badger your child to answer or rev up your frustration ("You are telling me you can't think of ONE good thing about today?"), and don't oversell the idea either.

Kids have an uncanny way of detecting when we parents are trying too hard, and the defenses kick in as they try to figure out what we are up to this time! Remember, relaxed equals ready when it comes to learning; don't give your child reasons to hold on tighter to that negative wheel.

Yes, it may take a while for your positive observations to sink in and become believable to your child. The change you notice on the outside may be small and inconsistent. Still, commenting on what is positive about your child is worthwhile. Pointing out what you love fills your child's self-esteem tank, buffering daily life from the drain of pessimism. As a parent, keeping a vigilant watch for your child's positives is helpful for you too! Parenting is way more relaxing when your assignment is to notice what you enjoy about your child every other minute of the day!

Strategy Three: Build the Opposite

Your child needs options when it comes to figuring out how to feel about a situation. Right now the bad details tend to pop up first, cutting off the positive or even "good enough" parts of the story. The strategies below will lay down more affirmative tracks and will direct the brain's attention to what is right about the day. And what is "right" doesn't have to mean positive or jolly; being able to even just tolerate a situation is much more useful than what your child's negative mind focuses on now. Just like the other ideas in this book, these require minimal effort or buy-in from your child.

So how to do you build the opposite of negativity? Focus on these three things:

1. **What I Like About You**

2. **What You Like About You**

3. **What Others See In You**

1. What I Like About You

Negative children can be as judgmental about themselves as they are about the world, especially as they get older. They believe that they will never be as good as they want to be at school, sports, hobbies, friendships, or jobs. As parents, we are in a prime position to teach them how to be grateful for who they are, flaws and all. To foster a more positive view of self for your child, you need to once again intentionally lay down the roadways that give the brain somewhere to exit on a bad day.

Try this: Establish a holding spot for pieces of gratitude.

Put a cup in your child's sock drawer, tuck an envelope under the bedroom pillow, or start a picture journal of the aspects of your child that you cherish. Comment in words or pictures on traits such as:

Creativity

Love of animals

Curiosity about the world

Willingness to ride the craziest roller coaster at the park

Amazing ease of connecting with others

Passion for old toys

Caring nature towards friends

Ethic of hard work

Love of trivia about a favorite movie

Ability to memorize useless but funny facts
Sticking to commitments
Organization skills
Time management

You will notice that every suggestion on this list involves character traits that your child can foster over a lifetime. Avoid too much praise for personal aspects that are mostly the product of genetics such as looks, smarts, or physical ability. You want your child to strive for the goals they can influence and not get stuck feeling like intelligence, beauty, and prowess are the only traits that matter to you or the world. Research by Carol Dweck and her colleagues have, in fact, found that praise focused solely on intelligence actually decreases a child's confidence and enjoyment in tackling problems once a task becomes hard. It is as if struggling somehow means that you are suddenly not smart. You can read more about Dr. Dweck's work on this topic and the importance of one's mindset in her book, *Mindset: The New Psychology of Success.*

The secret to the **What I Like About You** strategy is to add it to your first strategy of noticing daily positives. Unlike your **Good Thing of The Day** comments described above, expressions of gratitude are meant to convey your love of the enduring parts of your child that persist through the ups and downs of a day, week, or year. You might get mad at your significant other for forgetting to run to the store, but you are still grateful to share a good laugh over your favorite late night show. The same no-matter-what connections are valued by your child as well. Rewire your child and your-self to notice that the people we love are more than their grumpy days or grouchy moments.

Commit to the daily habit of noticing the opposite of what's exasperating about your child.

Therapist Note: The journey of gratitude sometimes seems long and unrewarding to parents. Kids rarely seem to appreciate the kind words and any impact on behavior is hard to identify. Being grateful for your child and putting it in writing is still worth it. Many youngsters in my clinic tell me they look forward to seeing new slips of paper with comments from their parents about something special they just don't see in themselves. They dump out the pile of compliments on their bed and read through them when they are feeling down.

Those comments matter. And they encourage your child to keep trying. And they help your child rewrite the story they tell about themselves. Even if you never hear about it!

2. What You Like About You

A well-known strategy in psychology for improving self-esteem is engaging in things you are good at as often as possible. When you have an emotional bank account filled with deposits of success, accomplishment, and satisfaction, it is easier to be positive about the world around you. If your child is feeling confident about small, shining moments throughout the day, messages of negativity have to compete for room on the road, weakening the hold those messages have on the wheel.

What if you or your child doesn't know what qualities are hiding in that beautiful brain? Below are some ideas to help figure it out:

    A. Encourage your child to master age-appropriate skills.

    B. Provide resources to promote a talent.

    C. Create an environment of acceptance.

A. Master skills: One way to help your child build evidence that the negative voice isn't always right is to encourage the mastery of age-appropriate skills. Why? Negative children are often unintentionally trained to be helpless. It can be easier for parents to just do a task ourselves than to deal with the hassle of a whiny, complaining child. If you give up on your requests for putting away clothes or hanging up wet towels, this may be the message you are sending: "I don't believe you are capable of doing this, so I'm just going to do it myself." A vicious cycle of requesting, resistance, and giving up repeats over and over again. Or, you don't even ask, your child doesn't get to learn, and you get frustrated that your child does not have a skill.

Negative children, more than others, truly need experiences of accomplishment to help lay down a road of confidence when doubt and distrust are bossing them around. Starting where you need to start is essential here.

Another tip for building confidence is to start with tasks your child already enjoys. Your child may be willing to organize a favorite movie collection or help rake leaves if it means a big pile to jump into later. Or maybe you can start with allowing your child to add the snack to school lunch every day, then slowly add in fixing a water bottle or choosing a fruit. Older kids might be more willing to use a checklist to make sure they have everything they need in their sports bag even if they resist packing their backpack for school. As they get better at packing for extracurricular activities, have them help you problem solve ways to apply their organizational talents to packing for school.

These ideas can apply to any aspect of your child's daily life that would fall under the "chore" category. At my house, even though my kids "can" clean their rooms, we often tackle it together. We crank some music, divide the room into zones, and get to work. I am confident my kids will be able to clean on their own by the time they move away from home. Why? Because they are learning how to clean under relaxed conditions, with lots of practice picking up without a showdown of what they "should" be able to do by their age. I know it may not seem ideal to have to hand-hold your child's skill building this much. But what do you have now? You are exhausted from doing too much and irritable every night as you fume over how your child ignored or fussed about your requests.

The bottom line is that it is more important to slowly build confidence and cooperation than it is to master a specific skill. In other words, a pleasant chat while you help your child pack a sack lunch is much more effective for advancing independence than a belittling lecture about how your child "should" be able to get it done alone. Parenting is a marathon and it is smart to pace yourself. You have many years to help your child become self-sufficient away from your care.

B. Promote a Talent: As a parent, it is probably easy to see how encouraging your child's strengths and talents are necessary for self-esteem! Options are available in most communities to explore talents like sports, dance, music, art, theatre, and computer sciences. In your own home, your child could learn to bake, organize, or make small home repairs. Expensive lessons and organized clubs are not needed. Merely dedicating some of your time and creativity to your child's passion will validate that what is important to your child is important to you. Without saying a word of praise or criticism, you can bank meaningful minutes in your child's day by spending time baking a new recipe or experimenting with a new form of goo. Don't forget to encourage the less-celebrated strengths in your child as well, such as organization and kindness. Opportunities to develop these types of traits might include putting your child in charge of a family project or volunteering together regularly at an animal shelter. One family I know takes turns challenging family members to make something seen on Pinterest and then enjoys an evening full of laughter at the "fails".

If your child seems short on interests or perceived strengths, consider engaging friends, family members, or teachers in the hunt for a passion or to reinforce what is great about your kid. Perhaps a neighbor is an excellent crafter, or a grandparent knows how to woodwork. See if they will let your child tag along as a helper. Maybe an aunt could share some ideas for origami or tablet apps that require creative thinking skills. A teacher could need some help organizing a classroom. A friend's interest in a sport could encourage your child to sign up for the same team or to take an art class together. Yes, there is some risk in the negativity monster resisting such new territory, but if you thoughtfully start with expanding already-preferred activities, enlist the help of others, and have no significant emotional investment in the outcome, your child's curiosity and desire to accomplish may win the battle against negativity's resistance.

C. Create an Atmosphere of Acceptance: In my practice, I am sometimes asked by parents to help a child with "low self-esteem." As I interview the family, I hear parents belittle, correct or control most aspects of the child's life but then scratch their heads as to why their child does not have a positive self-image. If you redo your child's hair before leaving the house, criticize clothing choices, hover over every activity, and dissect every aspect of a basketball game or art project, you are destroying confidence, not building it. Confidence comes from being accepted for who you are and from being allowed to try some things your way, succeed or fail.

It is easier to like yourself when you are surrounded by others who accept you and share your interests. Think about what intrigues your child, even if it is not exciting to you. What can you do to start being more accepting of that interest? How about taking an art class together? What about actually watching basketball practice instead of burying your nose in your phone? If your child is an avid reader, start reading a series of chapter books together. Would your kid love it if you sat and watched a favorite show? How about trying to learn the nuances of the video game that is so intriguing to your child? Our local taekwondo studio offers free training for parents when they sign up their kids. What a literal kick to have your dad beside you learning how to do a step reverse side kick! You may have to work harder on this than other parents if your child's interests do not match yours. You may also have to advocate for your child if other family members try to tear down the interests they pursue.

Not every child is an athlete or musician or a math whiz. If you keep pushing in directions that only interest you, you can expect negativity and self-doubt to continue. I know it can take a while to figure out just what your child likes and I'm not suggesting to avoid every activity your child says "no" to or to quit at the first sign of resistance. I am saying, over time, pay attention to what your child likes and do everything you can to accept and nurture those desires.

3. What Others See In You

One of the best ways to feel better about ourselves is to shift our focus to others. If your child can get positive affirmation from other people, that self-esteem tank continues to fill. One of the best ways to solicit such positive feedback is to step outside of your family life and focus on the needs of others. Even if your child grumbles through the whole adventure, be confident that you are slowly creating an intriguing rest stop on that negative highway—a place to take a break from the stress and struggle of a bossy brain.

Here are some ideas to get you started:

Pick out toys and supplies to donate to a pet shelter.

Bring snacks to the local fire department.

Have your child make a picture as a "thank you" for the dentist.

Ask the school secretary to allow your child to secretly place a treat in the principal's mailbox.

Ask your child to pay attention to what a teacher likes (coffee, chocolate, gum) and surprise him with a small gesture related to that desire.

Participate in gift-giving campaigns for less-fortunate children in your community.

Have your child help you sort and deliver gently worn clothes to a local shelter.

Allow your child to pick out a few extra groceries to donate to a food bank — your child should be there when you drop them off.

Volunteer as a family at events that benefit causes you believe in (again, ignore the whining!).

Host a "clean up the neighborhood" party and invite friends to sweep driveways or pick up trash.

Secretly bring a neighbor's newspaper or trash cans up from the curb.

Have your child host a summer book exchange with friends or neighbors.

All of these activities provide the opportunity for your child to hear praise from others and to feel pleased about at least a small part of the day. If you have a negative child, it is more critical for your family than perhaps others to make time to engage in these types of giving activities. Negative people have a narrow definition of happy and don't need much supporting evidence to return to their misery. The more new adventures you go on, the more you break up those roadblocks and provide sneak peeks into other journeys. The steps don't have to be very big or far away, just frequent enough to wear a new path!

What can you commit to this month? Who could you delight in your child's life with a good deed (secret ones are always more thrilling!)? How could you help out in your neighborhood or community? What projects could you commit to every year to build a family tradition that benefits your child as much as those you are helping?

You are reading this book because you need strategies to help your child be more positive, even without cooperation. Being kind to others is unquestionably one of those strategies!

If the only ideas you try from this book are the ones from this chapter, you are on the right path to creating calm in your family. These ideas seem simple enough yet in reality are hard to remember and engage in every day. If you do nothing else, invest your efforts here. If you blow it and yell at your child for complaining, you can still circle back later and slip that gratitude note into its holding spot. After you beat yourself up for giving in whining, write down three positive traits about YOU and get back to your parenting work.

Every. Other. Minute. Your best work happens every other minute when you are not locked in a battle with negativity.

Negativity will not be the boss of your household anymore.

Now You Know

I am the Role Model for Handling Frustration. My Child is Watching

My Child will Learn to be More Positive if That is what I Focus On Every Day — In Words and On Paper

Encouraging My Child to Master Age-Appropriate Skills builds Confidence

My Child Deserves a Chance to Explore Interests

Doing for Others can Help My Child Notice the Positives in Life

The Most Important Parenting I Do is when Negative Emotions are Not in Charge

Chapter 5:

FAQ ABOUT NEGATIVITY

"So just how exactly do I handle THAT situation?"

There is no way one book can answer all of your questions or can predict every roadblock you might run into as you try your best to create a more positive journey for your child.

Some of the questions you might have asked yourself, just like the many parents I have seen over the years in my clinical practice, are in this chapter.

And my answers, crafted from training, experience, and mostly attributable to what I have learned from the kids and parents brave enough to seek help:

Question 1: Why is my child able to handle stress at school but not at home? The teachers never see this complaining, irritable grump of a child! Doesn't that mean that my child can be less pessimistic at home, but is just choosing not to?

Dr. V: Kids can be masters at holding in their negative feelings all day and then let loose as soon as they get in the car or off the bus. This skill doesn't mean their negative thoughts were leaving them alone, just that they followed the rules and social pressures of their environment like you do. You are unlikely to criticize your boss in a meeting, but will readily complain to your partner about what happened when you get home! You also pull out your best coping skills while at lunch with friends, even if you hate the restaurant or are bothered by the topics of conversation.

Just like adults, children absorb the stress of their experiences away from home and need a safe place to decompress. To help you child manage daily stress more effectively, consider calming activities like a bike ride, time to played with preferred toys, or even a little break with headphones and a movie if that is what your child needs to unwind and be ready to participate in your evening plans.

Avoid lots of questions about the day or homework. A simple, "Glad to see you!" and a hug can work wonders to help your child feel out from under the microscope. You may find that waiting a bit after school before making demands, and meeting your child's needs for food, exercise and downtime will decrease anxiety and negativity as the evening moves along. Of course, if you are concerned your child's stress is related to learning problems or mistreatment at school seek assistance from school personnel who can share their perspective and suggest options for further evaluation or support.

Question 2: When my child is upset, I try to convince him to look on the bright side. Why doesn't my reassuring work? Sometimes when I cheer my kid on, he gets even madder!

Dr. V: Of course there is a time and place for encouraging words and conversations about the sunny side. The trap of using them in response to negativity is that your child may be unable to truly consider those words in that moment and instead can feel like you don't understand. Think about a time you complained about an unfair situation at work. If your confidante immediately tells you how silly you are or how you should just be grateful you have a job, you would be rolling your eyes as you shut down, checking that person off of your list of useful listeners.

Save your comments and conversations about positivity for when your child is not in the middle of a negativity crisis and can actually take what you are saying to heart. When the road is clear, try saying something like, "I have been thinking about how that math test made you feel, and I'm wondering if we can come up with some ideas about what went wrong." Your child may then be open to ideas like studying more or recognizing that a lower-than-desired grade just meant the test was hard and was not a sign of stupidity like their negative brain claimed a few hours ago.

Question 3: Sometimes my child says incredibly scary words like, "I hate you" or "I hate myself" when faced with a consequence or a challenge. How should I respond when my child is that upset?

Dr. V: When children are upset, they often don't know how to put those feelings into words, except for the words that sound as horrible as they feel. Remember, when your child is emotional, the thinking brain is not in charge, so I would encourage you to say very little. Your words can be challenging to process and may just add to those big, scary feelings. Try calling it like it is, "I can tell you are super mad when you say those words" or "This problem is feeling so big right now," but don't try to manage those out-of-control feelings with language. Instead, help your child engage in calming activities. Put out a snack or drink, offer a hug or back rub (with permission), crank some music, or do some planks to send your child bursting into laughter. Now is not the time to lecture about respectful talk or to provide a long list of the reasons why your child is loved. Instead, take over the wheel and pull over to someplace safe.

Once the emotion has settled, maybe hours or even days later, your child might be open for a more productive talk on better options for expressing overwhelming feelings. Make a written list of stress busters to pull out when your child is mad, so neither one of you has to think on the spot of what might work. Kids need lots of options because although drawing might feel calming one day, a warm bath might do the trick the next time overwhelming feelings are in charge.

If, even after your best efforts your child still makes statements suggesting feelings of low self-worth, talk to your healthcare provider about a referral to a mental health specialist who can more carefully assess for mood disorders and give you and your child useful tools for communicating about intense emotions.

Question 4: My partner tells me I am just setting our child up for a hard life by clearing away everything that upsets her. I am just trying to live a day without a meltdown! He doesn't think we should avoid new restaurants or help with homework just because she is having a fit. Is he right?

Dr. V: Parenting a negative child is incredibly tough and caregivers often disagree on how to help. Yes, overindulging negativity by trying too hard to clear every pothole confirms your child's belief that unfairness and discomfort should be avoided at all costs. On the other hand, pushing your child to face every challenge — without consideration of just how overwhelming that can feel — feeds self-doubt and anxiety.

There is no "one-size-fits-all" answer to when you should push and when you should provide more support as a parent. One strategy that might help you sort out what to challenge and what to let go for now is to put your child's stressors on a visual ladder. If trying a new restaurant means a colossal meltdown 100% of the time, it's ok to take it off the list of experiences for now. Maybe trying a new ice cream shop instead would be a manageable place to start if dining out is important to your family. If doing homework without your help means hours of tears and fighting, it's ok to help. When your child is more confident, you can assist a little less. Or, hire a tutor who might be better able to get your child to do homework with less resistance. This can lay down those positive paths you are trying to develop to challenge your child's anxious desire to immediately exit when something is difficult. Then try again. You can't fight every battle — nor should you. Starting with ones your child can actually win builds confidence and a few exits on that negativity highway that will become more and more accessible with practice.

Question 5: What can I do to help other caregivers understand that yelling at our child when he is negative or upset just isn't helpful? I'm not perfect but I do know that arguing and threatening just makes things worse!

Dr. V: Parenting conflict can be very hard on relationships. Many adults are resistant to learning new ways of thinking about parenting, and they also default to anxious, negative responses when hitting a roadblock with their ornery offspring.

Try asking those caregivers to picture your child at the age of 21. How is that young person handling stress? Coping with challenges? Approaching new experiences? Does yelling, shaming, or modeling stubbornness grow that resilient, confident child you are looking forward to meeting in a few years? Be direct about the risks for an anxiety disorder or depression if harmful thinking habits are not addressed. Stay steady with how you approach your negative child so other caregivers can see the result — your child calms down more quickly when the adult isn't holding down the gas pedal.

Be careful not to address issues of parenting conflict when either you or the other caregiver is upset. Save your discussions for when you are both calm, your child is not in earshot, and preferably when you are out in public to encourage a polite exchange! Don't be afraid to seek family or individual therapy for more personalized strategies that fit the needs of your family. The wait for mental health services can be long, so look into finding a provider now. You can always cancel if your situation improves.

Question 6: In this book, you suggest that I agree with my child or ignore her when she is being negative. Doesn't that mean I am just giving in and saying that behavior is acceptable to me?

Dr. V: When you empathize with or ignore your child's negative emotions you are simply saying, "Sorry negativity (or anxiety), you aren't going to boss me around too!" You are modeling for your child how to stay calm in the face of stress. You are showing your child how to keep a response the right size. Over time, your child will come to trust that your reply is more accurate than what negativity has to say, and will then be more open to your stress-managing suggestions. For example, if your young child is complaining about having to come inside when she still wants to play, it is ok to say, "Yes, I know it is hard to leave something fun" while you take her hand to lead her inside. Or, if you have an older child who claims to hate his math class, empathize ("sounds like math is kicking your confidence right now") instead of launching into a long lecture about how helpful math will be in the future. The goal is to set your child up to regain emotional control and trust you; problem solving can come later.

Question 7: I have tried strategies like agreeing with my child or trying to be understanding and it just seems to create more anger! My child then gets sarcastic and says things like, "of course I am mad!" What should I do then?

Dr. V: As a parent, any time you try to change how you interact with your kids, there will likely be some pushback. Why? Because we humans like life to be predictable and filled with routine. If your child is used to you yelling or arguing in response to complaints, your shift to a more calm and understanding demeanor will feel weird and uncomfortable. As strange as it sounds, your child may push for a while to see if that familiar response of yours returns. The fancy term for this is an "extinction burst." Hang in there and stay calm. If your child does not like your comments, it's ok to say nothing. And it is best to not reply to those negative comebacks by adding more fuel with even sassier retorts. There is nothing to be gained by saying things like, "you are on your own then, I was just trying to help!" Again, your child needs to see that you are successfully resisting the path of negativity.

Question 8: You say that negative thinking can be a sign of anxiety or depression. How do I know if my child needs to be evaluated for these disorders?

Dr. V: If your parent alarm tells you that your child's mood problems are bigger than other kids of the same age, get those concerns checked out by a qualified professional. Start with your child's healthcare provider or ask for a referral to a mental health specialist. Your child's teacher might also be able to recommend credible local resources.

Here is some general information about anxiety and depression that can help you know what you are looking for when it comes to your child's mood:

Anxiety

A more worried response to a situation than you think is necessary given the circumstance:

Common worries:

> separation, weather, sleepovers, health and safety, social interactions, new experiences, specific phobias like heights or elevators

The response interferes with your child or your family's functioning:

> Missing school, tardy to school, can't attend crowded events, can't leave your child with a babysitter, have to reassure about safety repeatedly, won't try new activities

Your child has a difficult time controlling the anxious response:

> Cries, complains of frequent headaches or stomachaches, asks to come home from school or playdates, makes excuses, or refuses to participate in age-appropriate activities

Depression

Chronic irritability:

> Easily annoyed, quick to frustrate, snaps at even neutral comments

Loss of interest in activities:

> Doesn't want to play outside with friends, quits a beloved sport, passes on seeing a movie, finds fault in ordinarily fun events

Change in energy:

> Lethargic, keyed up, agitated

Changes in appetite:

> Always eating, loss of interest in food — even a favorite dessert isn't appealing

Changes in sleep:

> Can't fall asleep, wakes up a lot in the middle of the night, wants to sleep all the time

Makes comments that are hopeless or supercritical of oneself:

> "Why bother," "this is all my fault," "things never work out for me"
> Expresses a desire to hurt self or others

Of course, negative kids who are not depressed can be irritable, avoid putting energy into hard things, and can make self-defeating comments when upset about a demand or situation. If you feel your child also shares feelings of low self-worth even when not upset, or if you see other signs of depression as described above, please talk to a professional about your concerns.

It is better to err on the side of being an overly cautious parent in this case than to wait years and years with that knowing feeling in the pit in your stomach that something just isn't right with your child's mood. Worst case scenario when you seek help is that you learn some specific information about what to watch for and how to help your child cope with stress, even if it hasn't reached the level of a diagnosable disorder.

Still can't decide if you should seek help?

Here is a fact to consider: Most adults report having had symptoms of a mood problem for ten years before they got help.

A decade.

Don't let that be your child. Schedule an appointment to get some help.

Question 9: How do I know I am actually helping my child? It seems like my child is complaining less in some situations, but others are just as bad as before I started using the strategies in this book!

Dr. V: When it comes to parenting, sometimes it seems like the definition of success is a moving target! Please remember that time and practice are needed to master any new skill, and not getting bossed around by negativity is a skill. When something feels weird, kids default back to what feels comfortable — just like adults. You may be a pro at eating healthy when you are in the middle of a typical week, but throw in a long road trip or a health crisis for a family member, and you are back to eating whatever you can find to keep up your energy.

For children with a cynical nature, look for very small sightings of flexibility where there once was rigidity and screams of unfairness. Perhaps a sibling's bigger brownie or arrival at the front door first goes unnoticed or without a tantrum. Or maybe you hear your preteen tell a friend, "I am sure she must be busy, that is why she isn't texting us back right now" instead of the usual fortune-telling of a friendship crisis.

It is normal for your child (for all of us) to have good days and bad when it comes to our emotional regulation. If you are meeting your child at the skill starting line, keeping your expectations and own responses reasonable, and shoring up the minutes between disasters with positivity, you will be setting up your child to make great strides in emotional regulation.

Question 10: I get that I am an essential part of helping my child overcome negativity, but my child tells me she wants to learn more ways not to be so grouchy. When can I start teaching her how to help herself?

Dr. V: There is no magic age for teaching your child how to recognize and fight negativity. The most important factors to consider are how open your child is in general to your feedback, the level of current or chronic stressors in your home, any learning or attention problems for your child, and the priority of addressing negativity over other concerns you have for your child. You should also make sure that you are doing your part to clear the barriers in your home that might make it difficult for your child to practice positivity, like being reactive yourself. Your child will have a much harder time mastering coping skills if you are negative, volatile, or too demanding in your expectations.

One of my favorite resources for children ages 8-12 who want to learn some specific strategies for navigating negativity is, *"What to do When You Grumble Too Much"* by Dawn Huebner. Teenagers can learn more about their negative thinking habits and how to change them with the workbook, *"Conquer Negative Thinking for Teens: A Workbook to Break the Nine Thought Habits That Are Holding You Back"* by Mary Karapetian Alvord and Anne McGrath. When your child is ready, consider doing these workbooks together. You might learn some ideas for yourself too!

When you make it easier for your child to look for the positive, your confidence builds, your household breathes, and lifelong skills of resilience and flexibility take the wheel.

The time to navigate negativity is now!

For the latest information on parenting strategies and resources, visit Dr. Van Scoyoc's website at www.thetalkingdoc.com.

If you found this book to be useful, please leave an online review. Reviews like yours can make a huge difference in helping caregivers discover parenting books that really work. Imagine what all families could look like if negativity wasn't in charge!

With extraordinary gratitude,

Dr. V